I'm Glad I Have Siblings!

Written and Illustrated by
Dagmar Geisler

Translated by
Andrea Jones Berasaluce

Sky Pony Press
New York

We're Lucky to Have Siblings! Or Not?

"Sometimes I prayed that the baby would disappear," confessed one older brother when looking back.

Frustration can run so deep with a new sibling in the family! Dagmar Geisler does something very important in this book: she legitimizes such feelings. She often says these thoughts and feelings are normal, which offers a relief to those who experience them. Sometimes older siblings can feel rejected, even when it's actually love that's provided. "You must love your sibling," they often hear.

Yes, the experience of parents' attention needing to be divided is unpleasant; yes, being the "big" sibling is annoying. But it also has its upsides. Being the only child has advantages. Although . . .

Children who have had siblings for a long time or from birth paint a wonderfully varied picture. Throughout this book, they all offer their words of advice. And the chorus of experiences puts into perspective the aversion to the baby, of which the protagonist, Mira, often directly speaks. "Don't you see anything good in having a little brother?" asks Lilly.
"Sure. . . . He's pretty sweet" is what comes to Mira's mind.

Seen throughout the children's discussions are the author's empathetic statements carefully enhancing what the children say. The lion's share of the persuasive efforts, however, the children put forth themselves with their tales of big and little, of jealousy and love, similarity and difference. In the end, Ben gets the longed-for twin siblings and Theo, the naysayer, is convinced by the baby that he—maybe—made a mistake. The encounter seals the deal: the "little bawler" is sweet!

A thoroughly enjoyable, fun read with added value for the whole family.

Dr. Martina Steinkühler
Professor of Religious Pedagogy

Some of us have siblings.
How about you?

Over the holidays, Mira got a little brother. When she goes back to her play group, she tells her friends the news.

Many of them already have siblings. For example, Paul has a big sister. Hannah also has a big sister and a little brother, too. Ben, so far, doesn't have any siblings.

Amelie has two older siblings, but they live in a different city. Lilly wants a sister and maybe a brother, too. Or, even better, twins.

Theo doesn't want any brothers or sisters. None at all. And certainly not after he hears what Mira tells them.

I was very much looking forward to my little brother. Honest! When he was still in Mom's belly, I always cuddled up with her and I could sometimes hear how the little guy moved around. I was excited when Dad brought Mom to the hospital. Grandma babysat me and made me lots of pancakes, as many as I wanted. I was even allowed to stay up very late. "You're now the big sister," she said. I thought that was great. I also was happy when they came home with the little bawler. But I don't think it's so great anymore.

Grandma went back home, and Mom and Dad are constantly tired. And whenever they aren't tired, they have something to do: change diapers, feed the baby, put him to bed, dress him, undress him, rock him, cuddle with him and worry when he cries for a long time. And no one has time left for me. It totally stinks!

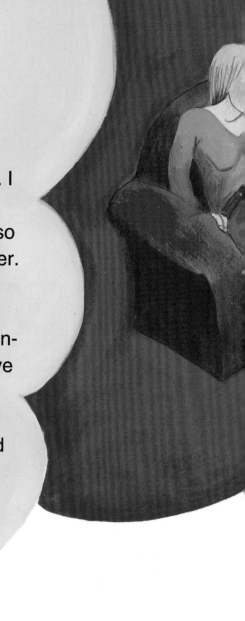

Mr. Schmitt

"Strongman" Robert

Mrs. Mayer

Ms. Flott

Officer Krause

No can remember being that small. But we were all once babies who needed help.

and MOM and DAD and GRANDMA and GRANDPA and AUNT and UNCLE and BROTHER and SISTER and... and...

And everyone has needed what all babies need.

Sometimes it can be really hard work, especially for the parents.

They also can't walk. You have to carry them everywhere.

Their stomachs are so small that they are often hungry.

Stomachache? Full diaper? Hungry? Or what?

They can't speak so they have to get by with screams.

. . . and all of this can happen even in the middle of the night.

"But not just for parents," says Mira.

"Don't you see anything good in having a little brother?" asks Lilly.

"Sure," says Mira. "He's pretty sweet, to be honest."

"Bah!" drones Theo and crosses his arms over his chest.

"Well," says Hannah. "Until my brother was born, I was always the smallest. When Aunt Susanne and Uncle Henry came to visit, they always said to me, 'Oh, how cute.' I thought that was pretty annoying. But once Hugo came, they said it to him and I found *that* really annoying."

"You're now the oldest," says Amelie.

But Hannah shakes her head. "No, that's my sister, Marie. She's the oldest."

"Cool," says Amelie. "Then you can always choose whether you want to be part of the older or the younger group."

"That's not a bad idea," thinks Hannah.

"Bah," drones Theo.

Paul would also like to be the oldest. Especially when his sister, Laura, is allowed to still stay up while he has to go to bed. Or when Mom and Dad are so excited that she can go for a ride with them on their huge bike. What can Paul do, since his legs aren't yet long enough to reach the pedals? And she can read really thick books all alone. And won't tell him what they say inside.

But sometimes, it's nice to be the younger one. Paul can still sit on Daddy's shoulders when the parades go by. Laura is sadly too heavy. Laura is afraid of thunderstorms, though, and often hides during them. Paul likes to protect her then. "I'm almost not scared at all when there's lightning and thunder," he says proudly.

"Bah," drones Theo. He also has no fear of lightning and thunder. But what does it matter?

Lena

Marty

Amelie has a big brother and a big sister. Both of them live with their mother in another city. Daddy got married for the second time to Amelie's mother. Amelie lives with her parents in a large house that has enough room for all the children.

Amelie likes it when Lena and Marty come to visit.

She has the coolest older sister in the world, Amelie thinks, and it's too bad that they rarely see each other. Only sometimes and only when no one can see, Amelie sticks her tongue out at Lena. She does this mainly when Daddy takes Lena in his arms and says how proud he is of his eldest.

"Bah," drones Theo. "That's much too stressful for me. Why do you need siblings at all? They only cause trouble."

"That's not true!" shout Amelie, Paul, and Hannah together. There are also a lot of good things that you miss out on if you don't have any brothers or sisters.

"Bah," drones Theo.

Even Mira knows a few reasons she no longer wishes her little brother away: "He smells so good and he has tiny fingers with even tinier fingernails. When he scrunches up his face into a smile, you have to smile back right away. When he sleeps, he looks like a little angel. It's nice to hold him in my arms and to push his stroller. I like to be Mom's oldest and help Dad change diapers."

And best of all, the little bawler gets bigger every day. At some point, he'll be able to talk and run and eat by himself, and then there will be a bit more of Mom and Dad left over for Mira.

But she doesn't have to wait so long, because Mira is not a baby anymore. She has been able to speak for a while now, and therefore she can say: "A week without cuddling is enough! It's my turn now!"

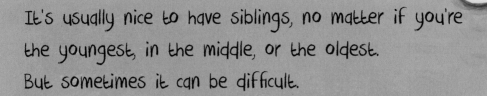

It's usually nice to have siblings, no matter if you're the youngest, in the middle, or the oldest.
But sometimes it can be difficult.

Luckily, you can talk about the challenges.

Sometimes you realize there wasn't much of a challenge to start. For example, you might talk yourself into believing that Mom and Dad don't love you as much now as they did before. Really, they're just distracted or awfully tired from caring so much for the new baby.

However, sometimes the challenge is real. Maybe because the baby gets all of your parents' attention, and it feels like they have no more time to snuggle or play with you.

It is helpful, if you're the older kid, to be patient. But if you have been very patient, you can talk to your parents about what's bothering you.

Sometimes it may feel like you can't talk about what's bothering you, either because you're not sure if it's a big deal or because you don't think anyone will listen. But keeping those feelings inside, and being angry or hurt without anyone knowing, is not a good idea. Because then the anger only grows and leads to a silly fight.

The good thing is, by talking to each other, you can find a solution. No matter what the problem.

A truly good idea is to arrange a time during which each person (Mom or Dad or siblings or friends) can say what annoys him/her and what makes him/her happy.

You don't have to always call me the little bawler. My name's Jakob.

Mira and her parents make time to talk every Friday, right before dinner. As he gets older, the little bawler will also speak up. What will he have to say?

When Mira brings Jakob to the play group the following week, he is still too small to be able to speak.

Lilly squeaks: "Oh, he's sweet."

Hannah smiles and says: "He looks like you, Mira."

"Bah," drones Theo.

Paul says: "If he wants, he can ride my bike later."

Then, unexpectedly, Theo asks: "May I hold him?"

"Oh, I forgot to tell you all! I'm getting siblings too," Ben says. "A boy and a girl."

"Twins?" asks Lilly, jealous. "How cool!"

"Bah," drones Theo. But it sounds almost a bit like he is as jealous as Lilly.

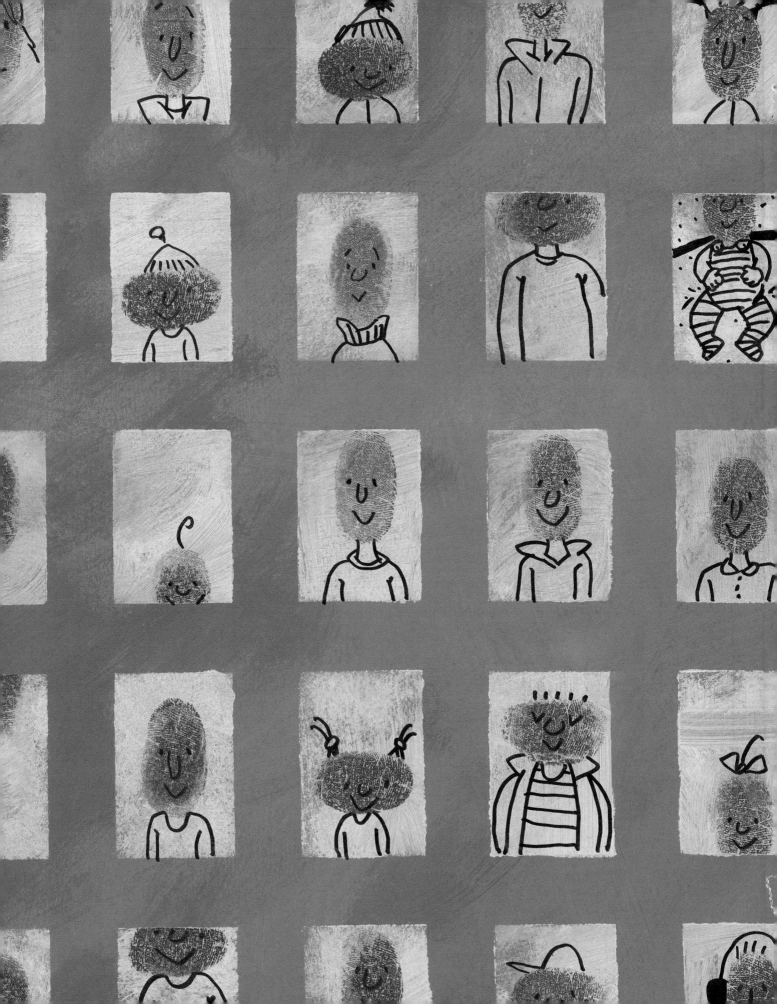